NEW EDITION

DIVINE MIRACLES WITH A DIVINE PURPOSE

THE
MIRACLES
^{OF}JESUS CHRIST
AND HIS APOSTLES

Alfred Cherubim

The Miracles of Jesus Christ and His Apostles

Alfred Cherubim

2023 © by Alfred Cherubim

All rights reserved. Published 2023.

BIBLE SCRIPTURES

Printed in the United States of America

Spirit Media and our logos are trademarks of Spirit Media

SPIRIT MEDIA
www.spiritmedia.us
1249 Kildaire Farm Rd STE 112
Cary, NC 27511
1 (888) 800-3744

Kindle eBooks | Religion & Spirituality | Christian Books & Bibles

eBook ISBN: 978-1-961614-51-2
Paperback ISBN: 978-1-961614-95-6
Hardback ISBN:978-1-961614-90-1
Audiobook ISBN: 978-1-961614-54-3
Library of Congress Control Number: 2023916720

Table of Contents

Divine Miracles with a Divine Purpose

Jesus performed mighty miracles when He was in this world.

"Jesus came to Nazareth, where he had been brought up; and, as his custom was, he went into the synagogue on the sabbath day, and stood up to read. The scroll of the prophet Isaiah was handed to Jesus. He opened the scroll and found the place where it was written, "The Spirit of the Lord is on me, because He has anointed me to proclaim good news to the poor. He has sent me to release the captives, restore sight to the blind, deliver those who are crushed, and to proclaim the acceptable year of the Lord." He closed the scroll, gave it back to the attendant, and sat down. The eyes of all in the synagogue were fastened on him. And He began to say unto them, This day is this scripture fulfilled in your ears." **Luke 4:16-21 (NIV)**

1

As these passages indicate, Jesus introduced Himself and the fact that He had arrived in full power and glory. Great things were about to be spoken and done in Israel and to those called to know and understand the miracles of Jesus, increasing our faith in God in the process. In these pages, the Bible lessons on miracles will enlighten you to the principles, purposes, and great powers of God Almighty. After a thorough study of His miracles, will you trust in God like never before you even believe in miracles? I hope so, because all of these miracles of Jesus Christ have many witnesses. Really, if you think about it, isn't it easy to believe in miracles if the Lord already created the universe by His word? For instance, He created man and woman, so, isn't it natural to believe He can heal them of any disease?

During His earthly ministry, Jesus Christ touched and transformed countless lives. Like other events in the life of Jesus, His miracles were documented by eyewitnesses. The four Gospels record thirty-seven miracles of Jesus, with Mark's Gospel recording the highest number.

Beyond each Gospel writer's accounts, Jesus' miracles were witnessed by multitudes of people who were made whole by our Savior. The closing verse of John's Gospel explains:

"Jesus did many other things as well. If every one of them were written down, I suppose that even the whole world would not have room for the books that would be written," **John 21:25 (NIV)**.

The thirty-seven miracles of Jesus Christ that were written down in the New Testament serve a specific purpose. None were performed randomly, for amusement, or for show. Each was accompanied by a message and either met a serious human need or confirmed Christ's identity and authority as the Son of God. At times, Jesus refused to perform miracles because they did not fall into one of these two categories:

"When Herod saw Jesus, he was very glad, for he had long desired to see him, because he had heard about him, and he was hoping to see some sign done by him. So he questioned him at some length, but he made no answer," **Luke 23:8–9 (ESV)**.

In the New Testament, three words refer to miracles:

- **Power** (*dynamis*), which means "mighty deed";

- **Sign** (*sēmeion*), which refers to a miracle that figuratively represents something else, such as the kingdom of God;

- **Wonder** (*teras*), which indicates something extraordinary.

Sometimes Jesus called on God, the Father, when performing miracles, and at other times He acted on His own authority, revealing both the Trinity and His individual divinity.

The First Miracle of Jesus

When Jesus turned water into wine at the wedding feast at Cana, He performed His first "miraculous sign," as the Gospel writer, John, called it. This miracle, showing Jesus' supernatural control over physical elements like water, revealed His glory as the Son of God and marked the beginning of His public ministry.

Some of Jesus' most astonishing miracles included raising people from the dead, restoring sight to the blind, casting out demons, healing the sick, and walking on water. All of Christ's miracles provided dramatic and clear evidence that He is the Son of God, validating His claim to the world.

Below, you will find a list of the miracles of Jesus depicted in the New Testament, along with corresponding Bible passages. These supernatural acts of love and power drew people to Jesus, revealed His divine nature, opened hearts to the message of salvation, and caused many to glorify God.

These signs and wonders demonstrated Christ's absolute power and authority over nature and His limitless compassion, proving that He was, indeed, the promised Messiah.

Join me as we closely look at all the miracles of Jesus and bring glory to God in the process.

37 Miracles of Jesus in Chronological Order

As much as possible, these miracles of Jesus Christ are presented in chronological order.

Thirty-Seven Miracles of Jesus					
#	Miracle		Mark	Luke	John
1	Jesus Turned Water into Wine at the Wedding Feast at Cana				2:1-11
2	Jesus Heals an Official's Son at Capernaum in Galilee				4:43-54
3	Jesus Drives Out an Evil Spirit from a Man in Capernaum		1:21-28	4:31-37	
4	Jesus Heals Peter's Mother-in-Law Who Was Sick with Fever	8:14-15	1:29-31	4:38-39	
5	Jesus Heals Many Sick and Oppressed by Evening	8:16-17	1:32-34	4:40-41	
6	First Miraculous Catch of Fish on the Lake of Gennesaret			5:1-11	

7	Jesus Cleanses a Man With Leprosy	8:1-4	1:40-45	5:12-14	
8	Jesus Heals a Centurion's Paralyzed Servant in Capernaum	8:5-13		7:1-10	
9	Jesus Heals a Paralytic Who Was Let Down from the Roof	9:1-8	2:1-12	5:17-26	
10	Jesus Heals a Man's Withered Hand on the Sabbath	12:9-14	3:1-6	6:6-11	
11	Jesus Raises a Widow's Son from the Dead in Nain			7:11-17	
12	Jesus Calms a Raging Storm on the Sea	8:23-27	4:35-41	8:22-25	
13	Jesus Casts Demons into a Herd of Pigs	8:28-33	5:1-20	8:26-39	
14	Jesus Heals a Woman in the Crowd with an Issue of Blood	9:20-22	5:25-34	8:42-48	
15	Jesus Raises Jairus' Daughter Back to Life	9:18, 23-26	5:21-24, 35-43	8:40-42, 49-56	
16	Jesus Heals Two Blind Men	9:27-31			
17	Jesus Heals a Man Who Was Unable to Speak	9:32-34			
18	Jesus Heals an Invalid at Bethesda				5:1-15
19	Jesus Feeds 5,000-Plus Women and Children	14:13-21	6:30-44	9:10-17	6:1-15
20	Jesus Walks on Water	14:22-33	6:45-52		6:16-21

21	Jesus Heals Many Sick in Gennesaret as They Touch His Garment	14:34-36	6:53-56		
22	Jesus Heals a Gentile Woman's Demon-Possessed Daughter	15:21-28	7:24-30		
23	Jesus Heals a Deaf and Dumb Man		7:31-37		
24	Jesus Feeds 4,000-Plus Women and Children	15:32-39	8:1-13		
25	Jesus Heals a Blind Man at Bethsaida		8:22-26		
26	Jesus Heals a Man Born Blind by Spitting in His Eyes				9:1-12
27	Jesus Heals a Boy with an Unclean Spirit	17:14-20	9:14-29	9:37-43	
28	Miraculous Temple Tax in a Fish's Mouth	17:24-27			
29	Jesus Heals a Blind, Mute Demoniac	12:22-23		11:14-23	
30	Jesus Heals a Woman Who Had Been Crippled for Eighteen Years			13:10-17	
31	Jesus Heals a Man with Dropsy on the Sabbath			14:1-6	
32	Jesus Cleanses Ten Lepers on the Way to Jerusalem			17:11-19	
33	Jesus Raises Lazarus from the Dead in Bethany				11:1-45
34	Jesus Restores Sight to Bartimaeus in Jericho	20:29-34	10:46-52	18:35-43	

35	Jesus Withers the Fig Tree on the Road from Bethany		11:12-14		
36	Jesus Heals a Servant's Severed Ear while He is Being Arrested			22:50-51	
37	The Second Miraculous Catch of Fish at the Sea of Tiberias				21:4-11

01

Jesus Turns Water into Wine
at the Wedding in Cana

John 4: 43-54 (NIV) [43]After the two days he left for Galilee. [44](Now Jesus himself had pointed out that a prophet has no honor in his own country.) [45]When he arrived in Galilee, the Galileans welcomed him. They had seen all that he had done in Jerusalem at the Passover Festival, for they also had been there. [46]Once more he visited Cana in Galilee, where he had turned the water into wine. And there was a certain royal official whose son lay sick at Capernaum. [47]When this man heard that Jesus had arrived in Galilee from Judea, he went to him and begged him to come and heal his son, who was close to death. [48]"Unless you people see signs and wonders," Jesus told him, "you will never believe." [49]The royal official said, "Sir, come down before my child dies." [50]"Go," Jesus replied, "your son will live." The man took Jesus at his word and departed. [51]While he was still on the way, his servants met him with the news that his boy was living. [52]When he inquired as to the time when his son got better, they said to him, "Yesterday, at one in the afternoon, the fever left him." [53]Then the father realized that this was the exact time at which Jesus had said to him, "Your son will live." So he and his whole household believed. [54]This was the second sign Jesus performed after coming from Judea to Galilee.

Jesus Heals an Official's Son at Capernaum in Galilee

John 4:43-54 (NLT) ⁴³At the end of the two days, Jesus went on to Galilee. ⁴⁴He himself had said that a prophet is not honored in his own hometown. ⁴⁵Yet the Galileans welcomed him, for they had been in Jerusalem at the Passover celebration and had seen everything he did there. ⁴⁶As he traveled through Galilee, he came to Cana, where he had turned the water into wine. There was a government official in nearby Capernaum whose son was very sick. ⁴⁷When he heard that Jesus had come from Judea to Galilee, he went and begged Jesus to come to Capernaum to heal his son, who was about to die. ⁴⁸Jesus asked, "Will you never believe in me unless you see miraculous signs and wonders?" ⁴⁹The official pleaded, "Lord, please come now before my little boy dies." ⁵⁰Then Jesus told him, "Go back home. Your son will live!" And the man believed what Jesus said and started home. ⁵¹While the man was on his way, some of his servants met him with the news that his son was alive and well. ⁵²He asked them when the boy had begun to get better, and they replied, "Yesterday afternoon at one o'clock his fever suddenly disappeared!" ⁵³Then the father realized that that was the very time Jesus had told him, "Your son will live." And he and his entire household believed in Jesus. ⁵⁴This was the second miraculous sign Jesus did in Galilee after coming from Judea.

03

Jesus Drives Out an Evil Spirit
from a Man in Capernaum

Mark 1:21-28 (ESV) [21]And they went into Capernaum, and immediately on the Sabbath he entered the synagogue and was teaching. [22]And they were astonished at his teaching, for he taught them as one who had authority, and not as the scribes. [23]And immediately there was in their synagogue a man with an unclean spirit. And he cried out, [24]"What have you to do with us, Jesus of Nazareth? Have you come to destroy us? I know who you are—the Holy One of God." [25]But Jesus rebuked him, saying, "Be silent, and come out of him!" [26]And the unclean spirit, convulsing him and crying out with a loud voice, came out of him. [27]And they were all amazed, so that they questioned among themselves, saying, "What is this? A new teaching with authority! He commands even the unclean spirits, and they obey him." [28]And at once his fame spread everywhere throughout all the surrounding region of Galilee.

04

Jesus Heals Peter's Mother-in-Law Who Was Sick with Fever

Matthew 8:14-15 (NET) [14]Now when Jesus entered Peter's house, he saw his mother-in-law lying down, sick with a fever. [15]He touched her hand, and the fever left her. Then she got up and began to serve them.

Mark 1:29-31 (NLT) [29]After Jesus left the synagogue with James and John, they went to Simon and Andrew's home. [30]Now Simon's mother-in-law was sick in bed with a high fever. They told Jesus about her right away. [31]So he went to her bedside, took her by the hand, and helped her sit up. Then the fever left her, and she prepared a meal for them.

Luke 4:38-39 (NIV) [38]Jesus left the synagogue and went to the home of Simon. Now Simon's mother-in-law was suffering from a high fever, and they asked Jesus to help her. [39]So he bent over her and rebuked the fever, and it left her. She got up at once and began to wait on them.

Jesus Heals Many Sick and Oppressed by Evening

Matthew 8:16-17 (ESV) [16]That evening they brought to him many who were oppressed by demons, and he cast out the spirits with a word and healed all who were sick. [17]This was to fulfill what was spoken by the prophet Isaiah: "He took our illnesses and bore our diseases."

Mark 1:32-34 (NLT) [32]That evening after sunset, many sick and demon-possessed people were brought to Jesus. [33]The whole town gathered at the door to watch. [34]So Jesus healed many people who were sick with various diseases, and he cast out many demons. But because the demons knew who he was, he did not allow them to speak.

Mark 1:32-34 (NET) [32]When it was evening, after sunset, they brought to him all who were sick and demon-possessed. [33]The whole town gathered by the door. [34]So he healed many who were sick with various diseases and drove out many demons. But he would not permit the demons to speak, because they knew him.

06

First Miraculous Catch of
Fish on the Lake of Gennesaret

Luke 5:1-11 (NIV) [1]One day as Jesus was standing by the Lake of Gennesaret, the people were crowding around him and listening to the word of God. [2]He saw at the water's edge two boats, left there by the fishermen, who were washing their nets. [3]He got into one of the boats, the one belonging to Simon, and asked him to put out a little from shore. Then he sat down and taught the people from the boat.

[4]When he had finished speaking, he said to Simon, "Put out into deep water, and let down the nets for a catch."

[5]Simon answered, "Master, we've worked hard all night and haven't caught anything. But because you say so, I will let down the nets."

[6]When they had done so, they caught such a large number of fish that their nets began to break. [7]So they signaled their partners in the other boat to come and help them, and they came and filled both boats so full that they began to sink.

⁸When Simon Peter saw this, he fell at Jesus' knees and said, "Go away from me, Lord; I am a sinful man!" ⁹For he and all his companions were astonished at the catch of fish they had taken, ¹⁰and so were James and John, the sons of Zebedee, Simon's partners.

Then Jesus said to Simon, "Don't be afraid; from now on you will fish for people." ¹¹So they pulled their boats up on shore, left everything and followed him.

07

Jesus Cleanses a Man with Leprosy

Matthew 8:1-4 (ESV) [1]When he came down from the mountain, great crowds followed him. [2]And behold, a leper came to him and knelt before him, saying, "Lord, if you will, you can make me clean." [3]And Jesus stretched out his hand and touched him, saying, "I will; be clean." And immediately his leprosy was cleansed. [4]And Jesus said to him, "See that you say nothing to anyone, but go, show yourself to the priest and offer the gift that Moses commanded, for a proof to them."

Mark 1:40-45 (NET) [40]Now a leper came to him and fell to his knees, asking for help. "If you are willing, you can make me clean," he said. [41]Moved with indignation, Jesus stretched out his hand and touched him, saying, "I am willing. Be clean!" [42]The leprosy left him at once, and he was clean. [43]Immediately Jesus sent the man away with a very strong warning. [44] He told him, "See that you do not say anything to anyone, but go, show yourself to a priest, and bring the offering that Moses commanded for your cleansing, as a testimony to them." [45]But as the man went out he began to announce it publicly and spread the story widely, so that Jesus was no longer able to enter any town openly but stayed outside in remote places. Still they kept coming to him from everywhere.

Luke 5:12-14 (NLT) [12]In one of the villages, Jesus met a man with an advanced case of leprosy. When the man saw Jesus, he bowed with his face to the ground, begging to be healed. "Lord," he said, "if you are willing, you can heal me and make me clean. [13]Jesus reached out and touched him. "I am willing," he said. "Be healed!" And instantly the leprosy disappeared. [14]Then Jesus instructed him not to tell anyone what had happened. He said, "Go to the priest and let him examine you. Take along the offering required in the law of Moses for those who have been healed of leprosy. This will be a public testimony that you have been cleansed."

08

Jesus Heals a Centurion's Paralyzed Servant in Capernaum

Matthew 8:5-13 (NIV) ⁵When Jesus had entered Capernaum, a centurion came to him, asking for help. ⁶"Lord," he said, "my servant lies at home paralyzed, suffering terribly."

⁷Jesus said to him, "Shall I come and heal him?"

⁸The centurion replied, "Lord, I do not deserve to have you come under my roof. But just say the word, and my servant will be healed. ⁹For I myself am a man under authority, with soldiers under me. I tell this one, 'Go,' and he goes; and that one, 'Come,' and he comes. I say to my servant, 'Do this,' and he does it."

¹⁰When Jesus heard this, he was amazed and said to those following him, "Truly I tell you, I have not found anyone in Israel with such great faith. ¹¹I say to you that many will come from the east and the west, and will take their places at the feast with Abraham, Isaac and Jacob in the kingdom of heaven. ¹²But the subjects of the kingdom will be thrown outside, into the darkness, where there will be weeping and

gnashing of teeth."

[13]Then Jesus said to the centurion, "Go! Let it be done just as you believed it would." And his servant was healed at that moment.

Luke 7:1-10 (ESV) [1]After he had finished all his sayings in the hearing of the people, he entered Capernaum. [2]Now a centurion had a servant who was sick and at the point of death, who was highly valued by him. [3]When the centurion[b] heard about Jesus, he sent to him elders of the Jews, asking him to come and heal his servant. [4]And when they came to Jesus, they pleaded with him earnestly, saying, "He is worthy to have you do this for him, [5]for he loves our nation, and he is the one who built us our synagogue." [6]And Jesus went with them. When he was not far from the house, the centurion sent friends, saying to him, "Lord, do not trouble yourself, for I am not worthy to have you come under my roof. [7]Therefore I did not presume to come to you. But say the word, and let my servant be healed. [8]For I too am a man set under authority, with soldiers under me: and I say to one, 'Go,' and he goes; and to another, 'Come,' and he comes; and to my servant, 'Do this,' and he does it." [9]When Jesus heard these things, he marveled at him, and turning to the crowd that followed him, said, "I tell you, not even in Israel have I found such faith." [10]And when those who had been sent returned to the house, they found the servant well.

09

Jesus Heals a Paralytic Who Was Let Down from the Roof

Matthew 9:1-8 (NET) [1]After getting into a boat he crossed to the other side and came to his own town. [2]Just then some people brought to him a paralytic lying on a stretcher. When Jesus saw their faith, he said to the paralytic, "Have courage, son! Your sins are forgiven." [3]Then some of the experts in the law said to themselves, "This man is blaspheming!" [4]When Jesus perceived their thoughts he said, "Why do you respond with evil in your hearts? [5]Which is easier, to say, 'Your sins are forgiven' or to say, 'Stand up and walk'? [6]But so that you may knowthat the Son of Man has authority on earth to forgive sins"—then he said to the paralytic—"Stand up, take your stretcher, and go home." [7]So he stood up and went home. [8]When the crowd saw this, they were afraid and honored God who had given such authority to men.

Mark 2:1-12 (NLT) When Jesus returned to Capernaum several days later, the news spread quickly that he was back home. ²Soon the house where he was staying was so packed with visitors that there was no more room, even outside the door. While he was preaching God's word to them, ³four men arrived carrying a paralyzed man on a mat. ⁴They couldn't bring him to Jesus because of the crowd, so they dug a hole through the roof above his head. Then they lowered the man on his mat, right down in front of Jesus. ⁵Seeing their faith, Jesus said to the paralyzed man, "My child, your sins are forgiven." ⁶But some of the teachers of religious law who were sitting there thought to themselves, ⁷"What is he saying? This is blasphemy! Only God can forgive sins!" ⁸Jesus knew immediately what they were thinking, so he asked them, "Why do you question this in your hearts? ⁹Is it easier to say to the paralyzed man 'Your sins are forgiven,' or 'Stand up, pick up your mat, and walk'? ¹⁰So I will prove to you that the Son of Man[a] has the authority on earth to forgive sins." Then Jesus turned to the paralyzed man and said, ¹¹"Stand up, pick up your mat, and go home!" ¹²And the man jumped up, grabbed his mat, and walked out through the stunned onlookers. They were all amazed and praised God, exclaiming, "We've never seen anything like this before!"

Luke 5:17-26 (NIV) ¹⁷One day Jesus was teaching, and Pharisees and teachers of the law were sitting there. They had come from every village of Galilee and from Judea and Jerusalem. And the power of the Lord was with Jesus to heal the sick. ¹⁸Some men came carrying a paralyzed man on a mat and tried to take him into the house to lay him before Jesus. ¹⁹When they could not find a way to do this because of the crowd, they went up on the roof and lowered him on his mat through the tiles into the middle of the crowd, right in front of Jesus.

[20]When Jesus saw their faith, he said, "Friend, your sins are forgiven."

[21]The Pharisees and the teachers of the law began thinking to themselves, "Who is this fellow who speaks blasphemy? Who can forgive sins but God alone?"

[22]Jesus knew what they were thinking and asked, "Why are you thinking these things in your hearts? [23]Which is easier: to say, 'Your sins are forgiven,' or to say, 'Get up and walk'? [24]But I want you to know that the Son of Man has authority on earth to forgive sins." So he said to the paralyzed man, "I tell you, get up, take your mat and go home." [25]Immediately he stood up in front of them, took what he had been lying on and went home praising God. [26]Everyone was amazed and gave praise to God. They were filled with awe and said, "We have seen remarkable things today."

10

Jesus Heals a Man's
Withered Hand on the Sabbath

Matthew 12:9-14 (ESV) [9]He went on from there and entered their synagogue. [10]And a man was there with a withered hand. And they asked him, "Is it lawful to heal on the Sabbath?"—so that they might accuse him. [11]He said to them, "Which one of you who has a sheep, if it falls into a pit on the Sabbath, will not take hold of it and lift it out? [12]Of how much more value is a man than a sheep! So it is lawful to do good on the Sabbath." [13]Then he said to the man, "Stretch out your hand." And the man stretched it out, and it was restored, healthy like the other. [14]But the Pharisees went out and conspired against him, how to destroy him.

Mark 3:1-6 (NET) [1]Then Jesus entered the synagogue again, and a man was there who had a withered hand. [2]They watched Jesus closely to see if he would heal him on the Sabbath, so that they could accuse him. [3]So he said to the man who had the withered hand, "Stand up among all these people." [4]Then he said to them, "Is it lawful to do good on the Sabbath, or evil, to save a life or destroy it?" But they were silent. [5]After looking around at them in anger, grieved by the hardness of their hearts, he said to the man, "Stretch out your hand." He stretched it out, and his hand was restored. ⁶So the Pharisees went out immediately and began plotting with the Herodians, as to how they could assassinate him.

Luke 6:6-11 (NLT) ⁶On another Sabbath day, a man with a deformed right hand was in the synagogue while Jesus was teaching. ⁷The teachers of religious law and the Pharisees watched Jesus closely. If he healed the man's hand, they planned to accuse him of working on the Sabbath. ⁸But Jesus knew their thoughts. He said to the man with the deformed hand, "Come and stand in front of everyone." So the man came forward. ⁹Then Jesus said to his critics, "I have a question for you. Does the law permit good deeds on the Sabbath, or is it a day for doing evil? Is this a day to save life or to destroy it?" ¹⁰He looked around at them one by one and then said to the man, "Hold out your hand." So the man held out his hand, and it was restored! ¹¹At this, the enemies of Jesus were wild with rage and began to discuss what to do with him.

11

Jesus Raises a Widow's Son from the Dead in Nain

Luke 7:11-17 (NIV) [11]Soon afterward, Jesus went to a town called Nain, and his disciples and a large crowd went along with him. [12]As he approached the town gate, a dead person was being carried out—the only son of his mother, and she was a widow. And a large crowd from the town was with her. [13]When the Lord saw her, his heart went out to her and he said, "Don't cry."

[14]Then he went up and touched the bier they were carrying him on, and the bearers stood still. He said, "Young man, I say to you, get up!" [15]The dead man sat up and began to talk, and Jesus gave him back to his mother.

[16]They were all filled with awe and praised God. "A great prophet has appeared among us," they said. "God has come to help his people." [17]This news about Jesus spread throughout Judea and the surrounding country.

12

Jesus Calms a Raging Storm on the Sea

Matthew 8:23-27 (ESV) [23]And when he got into the boat, his disciples followed him. [24]And behold, there arose a great storm on the sea, so that the boat was being swamped by the waves; but he was asleep. [25]And they went and woke him, saying, "Save us, Lord; we are perishing." [26]And he said to them, "Why are you afraid, O you of little faith?" Then he rose and rebuked the winds and the sea, and there was a great calm. [27]And the men marveled, saying, "What sort of man is this, that even winds and sea obey him?"

Mark 4:35-41 (NET) [35]On that day, when evening came, Jesus said to his disciples, "Let's go across to the other side of the lake." [36]So after leaving the crowd, they took him along, just as he was, in the boat, and other boats were with him. [37]Now a great windstorm developed and the waves were breaking into the boat, so that the boat was nearly swamped. [38]But he was in the stern, sleeping on a cushion. They woke him up and said to him, "Teacher, don't you care that we are about to die?" [39]So he got up and rebuked the wind, and said to the sea, "Be quiet! Calm down!" Then the wind stopped, and it was dead calm. ⁴⁰And he said to them, "Why are you cowardly? Do you still not have faith?" ⁴¹They were overwhelmed by fear and said to one another, "Who then is this? Even the wind and sea obey him!"

Luke 8:22-25 (NLT) ²²One day Jesus said to his disciples, "Let's cross to the other side of the lake." So they got into a boat and started out. ²³As they sailed across, Jesus settled down for a nap. But soon a fierce storm came down on the lake. The boat was filling with water, and they were in real danger. ²⁴The disciples went and woke him up, shouting, "Master, Master, we're going to drown!" When Jesus woke up, he rebuked the wind and the raging waves. Suddenly the storm stopped and all was calm. ²⁵Then he asked them, "Where is your faith?" The disciples were terrified and amazed. "Who is this man?" they asked each other. "When he gives a command, even the wind and waves obey him!"

13

Jesus Casts Demons into a Herd of Pigs

Matthew 8:28-33 (NIV) [28] When he arrived at the other side in the region of the Gadarenes, two demon-possessed men coming from the tombs met him. They were so violent that no one could pass that way. "What do you want with us, Son of God?" they shouted. "Have you come here to torture us before the appointed time?" Some distance from them a large herd of pigs was feeding. The demons begged Jesus, "If you drive us out, send us into the herd of pigs." He said to them, "Go!" So they came out and went into the pigs, and the whole herd rushed down the steep bank into the lake and died in the water. Those tending the pigs ran off, went into the town and reported all this, including what had happened to the demon-possessed men.

Mark 5:1-20 (ESV) They came to the other side of the sea, to the country of the Gerasenes. [2] And when Jesus had stepped out of the boat, immediately there met him out of the tombs a man with an unclean spirit. [3] He lived among the tombs. And no one could bind him anymore, not even with a chain, [4] for he had often been bound with shackles and chains, but he wrenched the chains apart, and he broke the shackles in pieces. No one had the strength to subdue him. [5] Night and day among the tombs and on the mountains he was always crying out and cutting himself with stones. [6] And when he saw

Jesus from afar, he ran and fell down before him. ⁷And crying out with a loud voice, he said, "What have you to do with me, Jesus, Son of the Most High God? I adjure you by God, do not torment me." ⁸For he was saying to him, "Come out of the man, you unclean spirit!" ⁹And Jesus asked him, "What is your name?" He replied, "My name is Legion, for we are many." ¹⁰And he begged him earnestly not to send them out of the country. ¹¹Now a great herd of pigs was feeding there on the hillside, ¹²and they begged him, saying, "Send us to the pigs; let us enter them." ¹³So he gave them permission. And the unclean spirits came out and entered the pigs; and the herd, numbering about two thousand, rushed down the steep bank into the sea and drowned in the sea.

¹⁴The herdsmen fled and told it in the city and in the country. And people came to see what it was that had happened. ¹⁵And they came to Jesus and saw the demon-possessed man, the one who had had the legion, sitting there, clothed and in his right mind, and they were afraid. ¹⁶And those who had seen it described to them what had happened to the demon-possessed man and to the pigs. ¹⁷And they began to beg Jesus to depart from their region. ¹⁸As he was getting into the boat, the man who had been possessed with demons begged him that he might be with him. ¹⁹And he did not permit him but said to him, "Go home to your friends and tell them how much

Luke 8:26-39 (NET) ²⁶So they sailed over to the region of the Gerasenes, which is opposite Galilee. ²⁷As Jesus stepped ashore, a certain man from the town met him who was possessed by demons. For a long time this man had worn no clothes and had not lived in a house, but among the tombs. ²⁸When he saw Jesus, he cried out, fell down before him, and shouted with a loud voice, "Leave me alone, Jesus, Son of the Most High God! I beg you, do not torment me!" ²⁹For Jesus had started commanding the evil spirit to come out of the man. (For it had seized him many times, so he would be bound with chains and shackles and kept under guard. But he would break the restraints and be driven by the demon into deserted places.) [30]Jesus then asked him, "What is your name?" He said, "Legion," because many demons had entered him. [31]And they began to beg him not to order them to depart into the abyss. [32]Now a large herd of pigs was feeding there on the hillside, and the demonic spirits begged Jesus to let them go into them. He gave them permission. [33]So the demons came out of the man and went into the pigs, and the herd of pigs rushed down the steep slope into the lake and drowned. [34]When the herdsmen saw what had happened, they ran off and spread the news in the town and countryside. [35]So the people went out to see what had happened, and they came to Jesus. They found the man from whom the demons had gone out, sitting at Jesus' feet, clothed and in his right mind, and they were afraid. [36]Those who had seen it told them how the man who had been demon-possessed had been healed. [37]Then all the people of the Gerasenes and the surrounding region asked Jesus to leave them alone, for they were seized with great fear. So he got into the boat and left. [38]The man from whom the demons had gone out begged to go with him, but Jesus sent him

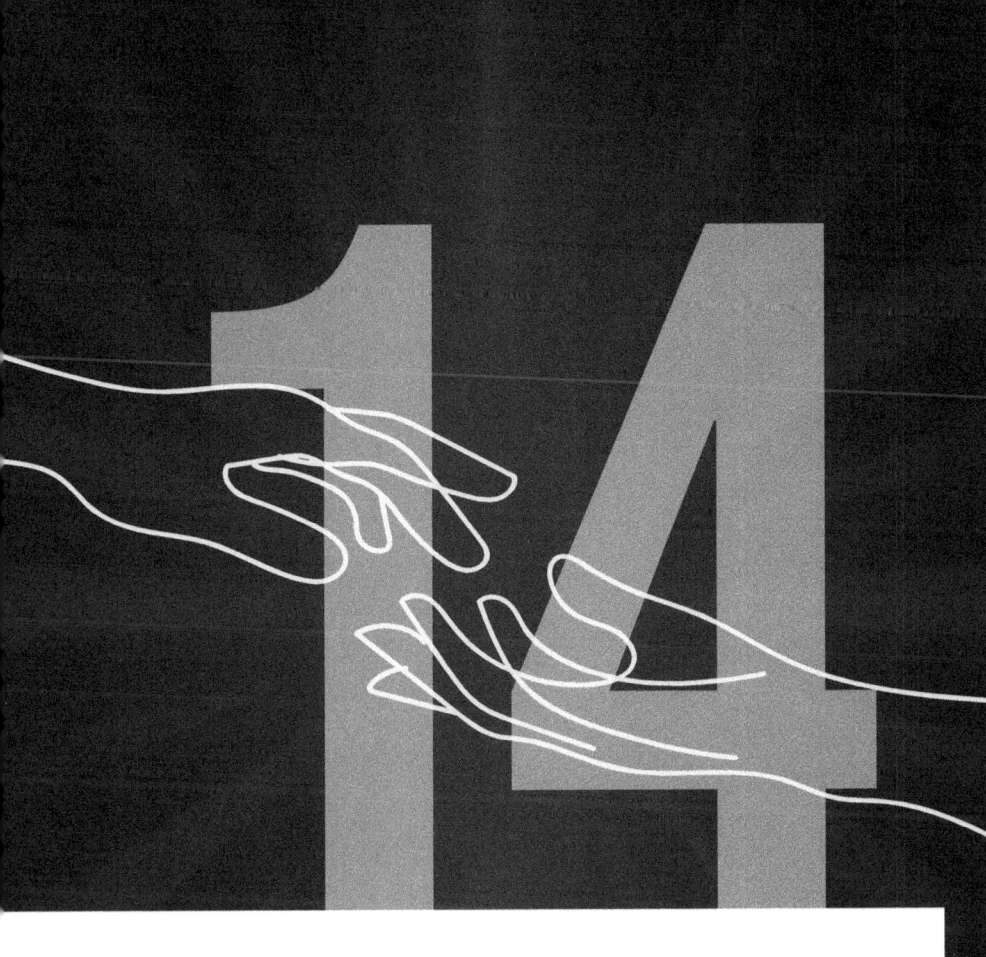

14

Jesus Heals a Woman in the
Crowd with an Issue of Blood

Matthew 9:20-22 (NLT) [20]Just then a woman who had suffered for twelve years with constant bleeding came up behind him. She touched the fringe of his robe, [21]for she thought, "If I can just touch his robe, I will be healed." [22]Jesus turned around, and when he saw her he said, "Daughter, be encouraged! Your faith has made you well." And the woman was healed at that moment.

Mark 5:25-34 (NIV) [25]And a woman was there who had been subject to bleeding for twelve years. [26]She had suffered a great deal under the care of many doctors and had spent all she had, yet instead of getting better she grew worse. [27]When she heard about Jesus, she came up behind him in the crowd and touched his cloak, [28]because she thought, "If I just touch his clothes, I will be healed." [29]Immediately her bleeding stopped and she felt in her body that she was freed from her suffering.

³⁰At once Jesus realized that power had gone out from him. He turned around in the crowd and asked, "Who touched my clothes?"

³¹"You see the people crowding against you," his disciples answered, "and yet you can ask, 'Who touched me?' "

³²But Jesus kept looking around to see who had done it. ³³Then the woman, knowing what had happened to her, came and fell at his feet and, trembling with fear, told him the whole truth. ³⁴He said to her, "Daughter, your faith has healed you. Go in peace and be freed from your suffering."

Luke 8:42-48 (ESV) ⁴²for he had an only daughter, about twelve years of age, and she was dying.

As Jesus went, the people pressed around him. ⁴³ And there was a woman who had had a discharge of blood for twelve years, and though she had spent all her living on physicians, she could not be healed by anyone. ⁴⁴She came up behind him and touched the fringe of his garment, and immediately her discharge of blood ceased. ⁴⁵And Jesus said, "Who was it that touched me?" When all denied it, Peter said, "Master, the crowds surround you and are pressing in on you!" ⁴⁶But Jesus said, "Someone touched me, for I perceive that power has gone out from me." ⁴⁷And when the woman saw that she was not hidden, she came trembling, and falling down before him declared in the presence of all the people why she had touched him, and how she had been immediately healed. ⁴⁸And he said to her, "Daughter, your faith has made you well; go in peace."

15

Jesus Raises Jairus' Daughter Back to Life

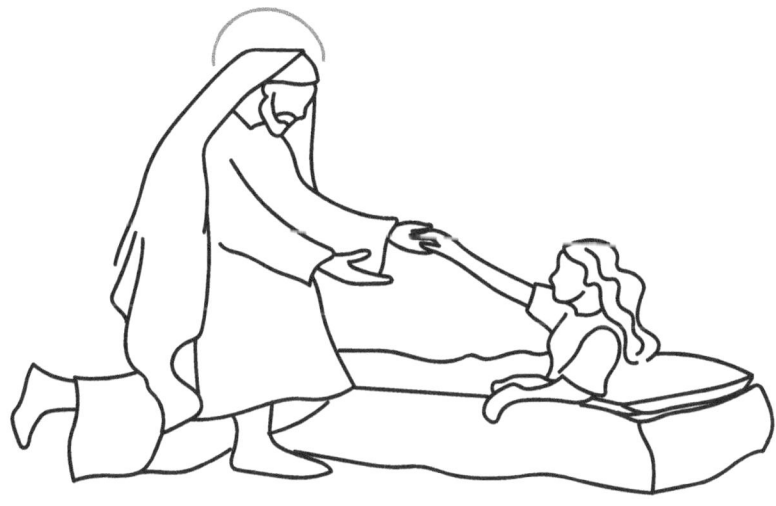

Matthew 9:18 (NET) ¹⁸As he was saying these things, a ruler came, bowed low before him, and said, "My daughter has just died, but come and lay your hand on her and she will live."

Matthew 9:24-26 (NIV) ²³When Jesus entered the synagogue leader's house and saw the noisy crowd and people playing pipes, ²⁴he said, "Go away. The girl is not dead but asleep." But they laughed at him. ²⁵After the crowd had been put outside, he went in and took the girl by the hand, and she got up. ²⁶News of this spread through all that region.

Mark 5:21-24 (ESV) ²¹And when Jesus had crossed again in the boat to the other side, a great crowd gathered about him, and he was beside the sea. ²²Then came one of the rulers of the synagogue, Jairus by name, and seeing him, he fell at his feet ²³and implored him earnestly, saying, "My little daughter is at the point of death. Come and lay your hands on her, so that she may be made well and live." ²⁴And he went with him. And a great crowd followed him and thronged about him.

Mark 5:35-43 (NET) ³⁵While he was still speaking, people came from the synagogue ruler's house saying, "Your daughter has died. Why trouble the teacher any longer?" ³⁶ But Jesus, paying no attention to what was said, told the synagogue ruler, "Do not be afraid; just believe." ³⁷He did not let anyone follow him except Peter, James, and John, the brother of James. ³⁸They came to the house of the synagogue ruler where he saw noisy confusion and people weeping and wailing loudly. ³⁹When he entered he said to them, "Why are you distressed and weeping? The child is not dead but asleep." ⁴⁰And they began making fun of him. But he put them all outside and he took the child's father and mother and his own companions and went into the room where the child was. ⁴¹Then, gently taking the child by the hand, he said to her, "*Talitha cumi*," which means, "Little girl, I say to you, get up." ⁴²The girl got up at once and began to walk around (she was twelve years old). They were completely astonished at this. ⁴³He strictly ordered that no one should know about this, and told them to give her something to eat.

Luke 8:40-42 (NLT) ⁴⁰On the other side of the lake the crowds welcomed Jesus, because they had been waiting for him. ⁴¹Then a man named Jairus, a leader of the local synagogue, came and fell at Jesus' feet, pleading with him to come home with him. ⁴²His only daughter, who was about twelve years old, was dying. As Jesus went with him, he was surrounded by the crowds

Luke 8:49-56 (NET) ⁴⁹While he was still speaking, someone from the synagogue ruler's house came and said, "Your daughter is dead; do not trouble the teacher any longer." ⁵⁰But when Jesus heard this, he told him, "Do not be afraid; just believe, and she will be healed." ⁵¹Now when he came to the house, Jesus did not let anyone go in with him except Peter, John, and James, and the child's father and mother. ⁵²Now they were all wailing and mourning for her, but he said, "Stop your weeping; she is not dead but asleep." ⁵³And they began making fun of him, because they knew that she was dead. ⁵⁴But Jesus gently took her by the hand and said, "Child, get up." ⁵⁵Her spirit returned, and she got up immediately. Then he told them to give her something to eat. ⁵⁶Her parents were astonished, but he ordered them to tell no one what had happened.

16

Jesus Heals Two Blind Men

Matthew 9:27-31 (NIV) ²⁷As Jesus went on from there, two blind men followed him, calling out, "Have mercy on us, Son of David!"

²⁸When he had gone indoors, the blind men came to him, and he asked them, "Do you believe that I am able to do this?"

"Yes, Lord," they replied.

²⁹Then he touched their eyes and said, "According to your faith let it be done to you"; ³⁰and their sight was restored. Jesus warned them sternly, "See that no one knows about this." ³¹But they went out and spread the news about him all over that region.

17

Jesus Heals a Man Who Was Unable to Speak

Matthew 9:32-34 (ESV) ³²As they were going away, behold, a demon-oppressed man who was mute was brought to him. ³³And when the demon had been cast out, the mute man spoke. And the crowds marveled, saying, "Never was anything like this seen in Israel." ³⁴But the Pharisees said, "He casts out demons by the prince of demons."

18

Jesus Heals an
Invalid at Bethesda

John 5:1-15 (NET) [1]After this there was a Jewish feast, and Jesus went up to Jerusalem. [2]Now there is in Jerusalem by the Sheep Gate[d] a pool called Bethzatha in Aramaic, which has five covered walkways. [3]A great number of sick, blind, lame, and paralyzed people were lying in these walkways. [5]Now a man was there who had been disabled for thirty-eight years. [6]When Jesus saw him lying there and when he realized that the man had been disabled a long time already, he said to him, "Do you want to become well?" [7]The sick man answered him, "Sir, I have no one to put me into the pool when the water is stirred up. While I am trying to get into the water, someone else goes down there before me." [8]Jesus said to him, "Stand up! Pick up your mat and walk." [9]Immediately the man was healed, and he picked up his mat and started walking. (Now that day was a Sabbath.)

¹⁰So the Jewish leaders said to the man who had been healed, "It is the Sabbath, and you are not permitted to carry your mat." ¹¹But he answered them, "The man who made me well said to me, 'Pick up your mat and walk.'" ¹²They asked him, "Who is the man who said to you, 'Pick up your mat and walk'?" ¹³But the man who had been healed did not know who it was, for Jesus had slipped out, since there was a crowd in that place.

¹⁴After this Jesus found him at the temple and said to him, "Look, you have become well. Don't sin any more, lest anything worse happen to you." ¹⁵ The man went away and informed the Jewish leaders that Jesus was the one who had made him well.

19

Jesus Feeds 5,000-Plus Women and Children

Matthew 14:13-21 (NIV) [13]When Jesus heard what had happened, he withdrew by boat privately to a solitary place. Hearing of this, the crowds followed him on foot from the towns. [14]When Jesus landed and saw a large crowd, he had compassion on them and healed their sick.

[15]As evening approached, the disciples came to him and said, "This is a remote place, and it's already getting late. Send the crowds away, so they can go to the villages and buy themselves some food."

[16]Jesus replied, "They do not need to go away. You give them something to eat."

[17]"We have here only five loaves of bread and two fish," they answered.

[18]"Bring them here to me," he said. [19]And he directed the people to sit down on the grass. Taking the five loaves and

the two fish and looking up to heaven, he gave thanks and broke the loaves. Then he gave them to the disciples, and the disciples gave them to the people. [20]They all ate and were satisfied, and the disciples picked up twelve basketfuls of broken pieces that were left over. [21]The number of those who ate was about five thousand men, besides women and children.

Mark 6:30-44 (ESV) [30]The apostles returned to Jesus and told him all that they had done and taught. [31]And he said to them, "Come away by yourselves to a desolate place and rest a while." For many were coming and going, and they had no leisure even to eat. [32]And they went away in the boat to a desolate place by themselves. [33]Now many saw them going and recognized them, and they ran there on foot from all the towns and got there ahead of them. [34]When he went ashore he saw a great crowd, and he had compassion on them, because they were like sheep without a shepherd. And he began to teach them many things. [35]And when it grew late, his disciples came to him and said, "This is a desolate place, and the hour is now late. [36]Send them away to go into the surrounding countryside and villages and buy themselves something to eat." [37]But he answered them, "You give them something to eat." And they said to him, "Shall we go and buy two hundred denarii[a] worth of bread and give it to them to eat?" [38]And he said to them, "How many loaves do you have? Go and see." And when they had found out, they said, "Five, and two fish." [39]Then he commanded them all to sit down in groups on the green grass. [40]So they sat down in groups, by hundreds and by fifties. [41]And taking the five loaves and the two fish, he looked up to heaven and said a blessing and broke the loaves and gave them to the disciples to set before the people. And he divided the two fish among them all. [42]And they all ate and were satisfied. [43]And they took up twelve baskets full of broken pieces and of the fish. [44]And those who ate the loaves were five thousand men.

Luke 9:10-17 (NET) [10]When the apostles returned, they told Jesus everything they had done. Then he took them with him and they withdrew privately to a town called Bethsaida. [11]But when the crowds found out, they followed him. He welcomed them, spoke to them about the kingdom of God, and cured those who needed healing. [12]Now the day began to draw to a close, so the twelve came and said to Jesus, "Send the crowd away, so they can go into the surrounding villages and countryside and find lodging and food, because we are in an isolated place." [13]But he said to them, "You give them something to eat." They replied, "We have no more than five loaves and two fish—unless we go and buy food for all these people." [14](Now about 5,000 men were there.) Then he said to his disciples, "Have them sit down in groups of about fifty each." [15]So they did as Jesus directed, and the people all sat down.

[16]Then he took the five loaves and the two fish, and looking up to heaven he gave thanks[ab] and broke them. He gave them to the disciples to set before the crowd. [17]They all ate and were satisfied, and what was left over was picked up—twelve baskets of broken pieces.

John 6:1-15 (NIV) [1]Some time after this, Jesus crossed to the far shore of the Sea of Galilee (that is, the Sea of Tiberias), [2]and a great crowd of people followed him because they saw the signs he had performed by healing the sick. [3]Then Jesus went up on a mountainside and sat down with his disciples. [4]The Jewish Passover Festival was near.

[5]When Jesus looked up and saw a great crowd coming toward him, he said to Philip, "Where shall we buy bread for these people to eat?" [6]He asked this only to test him, for he already had in mind what he was going to do.

[7]Philip answered him, "It would take more than half a year's wages to buy enough bread for each one to have a bite!"

[8]Another of his disciples, Andrew, Simon Peter's brother, spoke up, [9]"Here is a boy with five small barley loaves and two small fish, but how far will they go among so many?"

[10]Jesus said, "Have the people sit down." There was plenty of grass in that place, and they sat down (about five thousand men were there). [11]Jesus then took the loaves, gave thanks, and distributed to those who were seated as much as they wanted. He did the same with the fish.

[12]When they had all had enough to eat, he said to his disciples, "Gather the pieces that are left over. Let nothing be wasted." [13]So they gathered them and filled twelve baskets with the pieces of the five barley loaves left over by those who had eaten.

20

Jesus Walks on Water

Matthew 14:22-23 (ESV) ²²Immediately he made the disciples get into the boat and go before him to the other side, while he dismissed the crowds. ²³And after he had dismissed the crowds, he went up on the mountain by himself to pray. When evening came, he was there alone, ²⁴but the boat by this time was a long way from the land, beaten by the waves, for the wind was against them. ²⁵And in the fourth watch of the night he came to them, walking on the sea. ²⁶But when the disciples saw him walking on the sea, they were terrified, and said, "It is a ghost!" and they cried out in fear. ²⁷But immediately Jesus spoke to them, saying, "Take heart; it is I. Do not be afraid."

²⁸And Peter answered him, "Lord, if it is you, command me to come to you on the water." ²⁹He said, "Come." So Peter got out of the boat and walked on the water and came to Jesus. ³⁰But when he saw the wind, he was afraid, and beginning to sink he cried out, "Lord, save me." ³¹Jesus imme-

diately reached out his hand and took hold of him, saying to him, "O you of little faith, why did you doubt?" ³²And when they got into the boat, the wind ceased. ³³And those in the boat worshiped him, saying, "Truly you are the Son of God."

Mark 6:45-52 (NET) ⁴⁵Immediately Jesus made his disciples get into the boat and go on ahead to the other side, to Bethsaida, while he dispersed the crowd. ⁴⁶After saying goodbye to them, he went to the mountain to pray. ⁴⁷When evening came, the boat was in the middle of the sea and he was alone on the land. ⁴⁸He saw them straining at the oars, because the wind was against them. As the night was ending, he came to them walking on the sea, for he wanted to pass by them. ⁴⁹When they saw him walking on the water they thought he was a ghost. They cried out, ⁵⁰for they all saw him and were terrified. But immediately he spoke to them: "Have courage! It is I. Do not be afraid." ⁵¹Then he went up with them into the boat, and the wind ceased. They were completely astonished, ⁵²because they did not understand about the loaves, but their hearts were hardened.

John 6:16-21 (NLT) ¹⁶That evening Jesus' disciples went down to the shore to wait for him. ¹⁷But as darkness fell and Jesus still hadn't come back, they got into the boat and headed across the lake toward Capernaum. ¹⁸Soon a gale swept down upon them, and the sea grew very rough. ¹⁹They had rowed three or four miles when suddenly they saw Jesus walking on the water toward the boat. They were terrified, ²⁰but he called out to them, "Don't be afraid. I am here!" ²¹Then they were eager to let him in the boat, and immediately they arrived at their destination!

21

Jesus Heals Many Sick in Gennesaret as They Touch His Garment

Matthew 14:34-36 (NIV) [34]When they had crossed over, they landed at Gennesaret. [35]And when the men of that place recognized Jesus, they sent word to all the surrounding country. People brought all their sick to him [36]and begged him to let the sick just touch the edge of his cloak, and all who touched it were healed.

Mark 6:53-56 (ESV) [53]When they had crossed over, they came to land at Gennesaret and moored to the shore. [54]And when they got out of the boat, the people immediately recognized him [55]and ran about the whole region and began to bring the sick people on their beds to wherever they heard he was. [56]And wherever he came, in villages, cities, or countryside, they laid the sick in the marketplaces and implored him that they might touch even the fringe of his garment. And as many as touched it were made well.

22

Jesus Heals a Gentile Woman's Demon-Possessed Daughter

Matthew 15:21-28 (NET) [21]After going out from there, Jesus went to the region of Tyre and Sidon. [22]A Canaanite woman from that area came and cried out, "Have mercy on me, Lord, Son of David! My daughter is horribly demon-possessed!" [23]But he did not answer her a word. Then[d] his disciples came and begged him, "Send her away, because she keeps on crying out after us." [24]So he answered, "I was sent only to the lost sheep of the house of Israel." [25]But she came and bowed down before him and said, "Lord, help me!" [26]"It is not right to take the children's bread and throw it to the dogs," he said. [27]"Yes, Lord," she replied, "but even the dogs eat the crumbs that fall from their masters' table." [28]Then Jesus answered her, "Woman, your faith is great! Let what you want be done for you." And her daughter was healed from that hour.

Mark 7:24-30 (NLT) ²⁴Then Jesus left Galilee and went north to the region of Tyre. He didn't want anyone to know which house he was staying in, but he couldn't keep it a secret. ²⁵Right away a woman who had heard about him came and fell at his feet. Her little girl was possessed by an evil spirit, ²⁶and she begged him to cast out the demon from her daughter. Since she was a Gentile, born in Syrian Phoenicia, ²⁷Jesus told her, "First I should feed the children—my own family, the Jews. It isn't right to take food from the children and throw it to the dogs." ²⁸She replied, "That's true, Lord, but even the dogs under the table are allowed to eat the scraps from the children's plates." ²⁹"Good answer!" he said. "Now go home, for the demon has left your daughter." ³⁰And when she arrived home, she found her little girl lying quietly in bed, and the demon was gone.

Jesus Heals a Deaf and Dumb Man

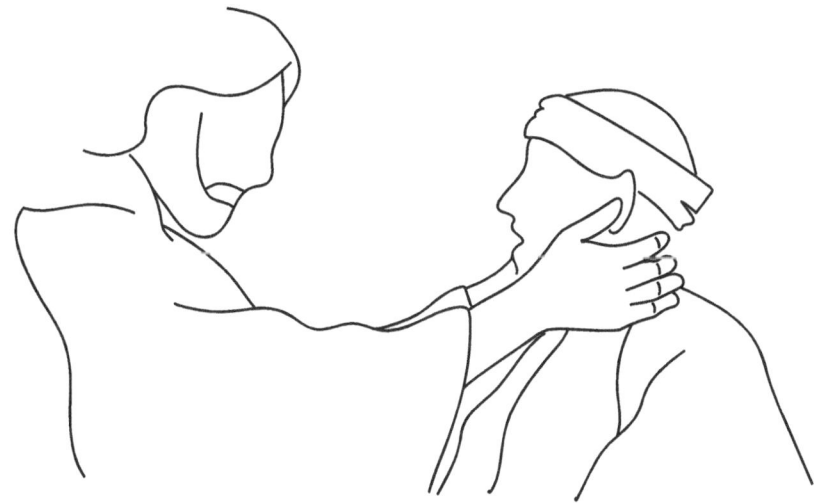

Mark 7:31-37 (NIV) [31]Then Jesus left the vicinity of Tyre and went through Sidon, down to the Sea of Galilee and into the region of the Decapolis. [32]There some people brought to him a man who was deaf and could hardly talk, and they begged Jesus to place his hand on him.

[33]After he took him aside, away from the crowd, Jesus put his fingers into the man's ears. Then he spit and touched the man's tongue. [34]He looked up to heaven and with a deep sigh said to him, "Ephphatha!" (which means "Be opened!"). [35]At this, the man's ears were opened, his tongue was loosened and he began to speak plainly.

[36]Jesus commanded them not to tell anyone. But the more he did so, the more they kept talking about it. [37]People were overwhelmed with amazement. "He has done everything well," they said. "He even makes the deaf hear and the mute speak."

24

Jesus Feeds 4,000-Plus Women and Children

Matthew 15:32-39 (ESV) [32]Then Jesus called his disciples to him and said, "I have compassion on the crowd because they have been with me now three days and have nothing to eat. And I am unwilling to send them away hungry, lest they faint on the way." [33]And the disciples said to him, "Where are we to get enough bread in such a desolate place to feed so great a crowd?" [34]And Jesus said to them, "How many loaves do you have?" They said, "Seven, and a few small fish." [35]And directing the crowd to sit down on the ground, [36]he took the seven loaves and the fish, and having given thanks he broke them and gave them to the disciples, and the disciples gave them to the crowds. [37]And they all ate and were satisfied. And they took up seven baskets full of the broken pieces left over. [38]Those who ate were four thousand men, besides women and children. [39]And after sending away the crowds, he got into the boat and went to the region of Magadan.

Mark 8:1-13 (NET) [1]In those days there was another large crowd with nothing to eat. So Jesus called his disciples and said to them, [2]"I have compassion on the crowd, because they have already been here with me three days, and they have nothing to eat. [3]If I send them home hungry, they will faint on the way, and some of them have come from a great distance." [4]His disciples answered him, "Where can someone get enough bread in this desolate place to satisfy these people?" [5]He asked them, "How many loaves do you have?" They replied, "Seven." [6]Then he directed the crowd to sit down on the ground. After he took the seven loaves and gave thanks, he broke them and began giving them to the disciples to serve. So they served the crowd. [7]They also had a few small fish. After giving thanks for these, he told them to serve these as well. [8]Everyone ate and was satisfied, and they picked up the broken pieces left over, seven baskets full. [9]There were about 4,000 who ate. Then he dismissed them. [10]Immediately he got into a boat with his disciples and went to the district of Dalmanutha.

25

Jesus Heals a Blind Man at Bethsaida

Mark 8:22-26 (NLT) ²²When they arrived at Bethsaida, some people brought a blind man to Jesus, and they begged him to touch the man and heal him. ²³Jesus took the blind man by the hand and led him out of the village. Then, spitting on the man's eyes, he laid his hands on him and asked, "Can you see anything now?" ²⁴The man looked around. "Yes," he said, "I see people, but I can't see them very clearly. They look like trees walking around." ²⁵Then Jesus placed his hands on the man's eyes again, and his eyes were opened. His sight was completely restored, and he could see everything clearly. ²⁶Jesus sent him away, saying, "Don't go back into the village on your way home."

26

Jesus Heals a Man Born Blind by Spitting in His Eyes

John 9:1-12 (NIV) [1]As he went along, he saw a man blind from birth. [2]His disciples asked him, "Rabbi, who sinned, this man or his parents, that he was born blind?" [3]"Neither this man nor his parents sinned," said Jesus, "but this happened so that the works of God might be displayed in him. [4]As long as it is day, we must do the works of him who sent me. Night is coming, when no one can work. [5]While I am in the world, I am the light of the world." [6]After saying this, he spit on the ground, made some mud with the saliva, and put it on the man's eyes. [7]"Go," he told him, "wash in the Pool of Siloam" (this word means "Sent"). So the man went and washed, and came home seeing. [8]His neighbors and those who had formerly seen him begging asked, "Isn't this the same man who used to sit and beg?" [9]Some claimed that he was. Others said, "No, he only looks like him." But he himself insisted, "I am the man." [10]"How then were your eyes opened?" they asked. [11]He replied, "The man they call Jesus made some mud and put it on my eyes. He told me to go to Siloam and wash. So I went and washed, and then I could see." [12]"Where is this man?" they asked him. "I don't know," he said.

27

Jesus Heals a Boy
with an Unclean Spirit

Matthew 17:14-20 (ESV) [14]And when they came to the crowd, a man came up to him and, kneeling before him, [15]said, "Lord, have mercy on my son, for he has seizures and he suffers terribly. For often he falls into the fire, and often into the water. [16]And I brought him to your disciples, and they could not heal him." [17]And Jesus answered, "O faithless and twisted generation, how long am I to be with you? How long am I to bear with you? Bring him here to me." [18]And Jesus rebuked the demon, and it came out of him, and the boy was healed instantly. [19]Then the disciples came to Jesus privately and said, "Why could we not cast it out?" [20]He said to them, "Because of your little faith. For truly, I say to you, if you have faith like a grain of mustard seed, you will say to this mountain, 'Move from here to there,' and it will move, and nothing will be impossible for you."

Mark 9:14-29 (NET) [14]When they came to the disciples, they saw a large crowd around them and experts in the law arguing with them. [15]When the whole crowd saw him, they were amazed and ran at once and greeted him. [16]He asked them, "What are you arguing about with them?" [17]A member of the crowd said to him, "Teacher, I brought you my son, who is possessed by a spirit that makes him mute. [18]Whenever it seizes him, it throws him down, and he foams at the mouth, grinds his teeth, and becomes rigid. I asked your disciples to cast it out, but they were not able to do so." [19]He answered them, "You unbelieving generation! How much longer must I be with you? How much longer must I endure you? Bring him to me." [20]So they brought the boy to him. When the spirit saw him, it immediately threw the boy into a convulsion. He fell on the ground and rolled around, foaming at the mouth. [21]Jesus asked his father, "How long has this been happening to him?" And he said, "From childhood. [22]It has often thrown him into fire or water to destroy him. But if you are able to do anything, have compassion on us and help us." [23]Then Jesus said to him, "'If you are able?' All things are possible for the one who believes." [24]Immediately the father of the boy cried out and said, "I believe; help my unbelief!"

[25]Now when Jesus saw that a crowd was quickly gathering, he rebuked the unclean spirit, saying to it, "Mute and deaf spirit, I command you, come out of him and never enter him again." [26]It shrieked, threw him into terrible convulsions, and came out. The boy looked so much like a corpse that many said, "He is dead!" [27]But Jesus gently took his hand and raised him to his feet, and he stood up.

[28]Then, after he went into the house, his disciples asked him privately, "Why couldn't we cast it out?" [29]He told them, "This kind can come out only by prayer."

Luke 9:37-43 (NLT) ³⁷The next day, after they had come down the mountain, a large crowd met Jesus. ³⁸A man in the crowd called out to him, "Teacher, I beg you to look at my son, my only child. ³⁹An evil spirit keeps seizing him, making him scream. It throws him into convulsions so that he foams at the mouth. It batters him and hardly ever leaves him alone. ⁴⁰I begged your disciples to cast out the spirit, but they couldn't do it." ⁴¹Jesus said, "You faithless and corrupt people! How long must I be with you and put up with you?" Then he said to the man, "Bring your son here." ⁴²As the boy came forward, the demon knocked him to the ground and threw him into a violent convulsion. But Jesus rebuked the evil spirit and healed the boy. Then he gave him back to his father. ⁴³Awe gripped the people as they saw this majestic display of God's power.

28

Miraculous Temple Tax in a Fish's Mouth

Matthew 17-24-27 (NIV) ²⁴After Jesus and his disciples arrived in Capernaum, the collectors of the two-drachma temple tax came to Peter and asked, "Doesn't your teacher pay the temple tax?" ²⁵"Yes, he does," he replied. When Peter came into the house, Jesus was the first to speak. "What do you think, Simon?" he asked. "From whom do the kings of the earth collect duty and taxes—from their own children or from others?" ²⁶ "From others," Peter answered. "Then the children are exempt," Jesus said to him. ²⁷"But so that we may not cause offense, go to the lake and throw out your line. Take the first fish you catch; open its mouth and you will find a four-drachma coin. Take it and give it to them for my tax and yours."

Jesus Heals a Blind, Mute Demoniac

Matthew 12:22-23 (ESV) [22] Then a demon-oppressed man who was blind and mute was brought to him, and he healed him, so that the man spoke and saw. [23] And all the people were amazed, and said, "Can this be the Son of David?"

Luke 11:14-23 (NET) [14] Now he was casting out a demon that was mute. When the demon had gone out, the man who had been mute began to speak, and the crowds were amazed. [15] But some of them said, "By the power of Beelzebul, the ruler of demons, he casts out demons!" [16] Others, to test him, began asking for a sign from heaven. [17] But Jesus, realizing their thoughts, said to them, "Every kingdom divided against itself is destroyed, and a divided household falls. [18] So if Satan too is divided against himself, how will his kingdom stand? I ask you this because you claim that I cast out demons by Beelzebul. [19] Now if I cast out demons by Beelzebul, by whom do your sons cast them out? Therefore they will be your judges. ²⁰But if I cast out demons by the finger of God, then the kingdom of God has already overtaken you. ²¹When a strong man, fully armed, guards his own palace, his possessions are safe. ²²But when a stronger man attacks and conquers him, he takes away the first man's armor on which the man relied and divides up his plunder. ²³Whoever is not with me is against me, and whoever does not gather with me scatters.

30

Jesus Heals a Woman Who Had Been Crippled for Eighteen Years

Luke 13:10-17 (**NLT**) ¹⁰One Sabbath day as Jesus was teaching in a synagogue, ¹¹he saw a woman who had been crippled by an evil spirit. She had been bent double for eighteen years and was unable to stand up straight. ¹²When Jesus saw her, he called her over and said, "Dear woman, you are healed of your sickness!" ¹³Then he touched her, and instantly she could stand straight. How she praised God! ¹⁴But the leader in charge of the synagogue was indignant that Jesus had healed her on the Sabbath day. "There are six days of the week for working," he said to the crowd. "Come on those days to be healed, not on the Sabbath." ¹⁵But the Lord replied, "You hypocrites! Each of you works on the Sabbath day! Don't you untie your ox or your donkey from its stall on the Sabbath and lead it out for water? ¹⁶This dear woman, a daughter of Abraham, has been held in bondage by Satan for eighteen years. Isn't it right that she be released, even on the Sabbath?" ¹⁷This shamed his enemies, but all the people rejoiced at the wonderful things he did.

31

Jesus Heals a Man with Dropsy on the Sabbath

Luke 14:1-6 (NIV) ¹One Sabbath, when Jesus went to eat in the house of a prominent Pharisee, he was being carefully watched. ²There in front of him was a man suffering from abnormal swelling of his body. ³Jesus asked the Pharisees and experts in the law, "Is it lawful to heal on the Sabbath or not?" ⁴But they remained silent. So taking hold of the man, he healed him and sent him on his way. ⁵Then he asked them, "If one of you has a child or an ox that falls into a well on the Sabbath day, will you not immediately pull it out?" ⁶And they had nothing to say.

32

Jesus Cleanses Ten Lepers on the Way to Jerusalem

Luke 17:11-19 (ESV) [11]On the way to Jerusalem he was passing along between Samaria and Galilee. [12]And as he entered a village, he was met by ten lepers,who stood at a distance [13]and lifted up their voices, saying, "Jesus, Master, have mercy on us." [14]When he saw them he said to them, "Go and show yourselves to the priests." And as they went they were cleansed. [15]Then one of them, when he saw that he was healed, turned back, praising God with a loud voice; [16]and he fell on his face at Jesus' feet, giving him thanks. Now he was a Samaritan. [17]Then Jesus answered, "Were not ten cleansed? Where are the nine? [18]Was no one found to return and give praise to God except this foreigner?" [19]And he said to him, "Rise and go your way; your faith has made you well."

33

Jesus Raises Lazarus
from the Dead in Bethany

John 11:1-16 (NET) The Death of Lazarus [1]Now a certain man named Lazarus was sick. He was from Bethany, the village where Mary and her sister Martha lived. [2](Now it was Mary who anointed the Lord with perfumed oil and wiped his feet dry with her hair, whose brother Lazarus was sick.) [3]So the sisters sent a message to Jesus, "Lord, look, the one you love is sick." [4]When Jesus heard this, he said, "This sickness will not lead to death, but to God's glory, so that the Son of God may be glorified through it." [5](Now Jesus loved Martha and her sister and Lazarus.) [6]So when he heard that Lazarus was sick, he remained in the place where he was for two more days. [7]Then after this, he said to his disciples, "Let us go to Judea again." [8]The disciples replied, "Rabbi, the Jewish leaders were just now trying to stone you to death! Are you going there again?" [9]Jesus replied, "Are there not twelve hours in a day? If anyone walks around in the daytime, he does not stumble, because he sees the light of this world. [10]But if anyone walks around at night, he stumbles, because the light is not in him." After he said this, he added, "Our friend

Lazarus has fallen asleep. But I am going there to awaken him." ¹²Then the disciples replied, "Lord, if he has fallen asleep, he will recover." ¹³(Now Jesus had been talking about his death, but they thought he had been talking about real sleep.) ¹⁴Then Jesus told them plainly, "Lazarus has died, ¹⁵and I am glad for your sake that I was not there, so that you may believe. But let us go to him." ¹⁶So Thomas (called Didymus) said to his fellow disciples, "Let us go too, so that we may die with him."

John 11:17-37 (NIV) Jesus Comforts the Sisters of Lazarus ¹⁷On his arrival, Jesus found that Lazarus had already been in the tomb for four days. ¹⁸Now Bethany was less than two miles from Jerusalem, ¹⁹and many Jews had come to Martha and Mary to comfort them in the loss of their brother. ²⁰When Martha heard that Jesus was coming, she went out to meet him, but Mary stayed at home. ²¹"Lord," Martha said to Jesus, "if you had been here, my brother would not have died. ²²But I know that even now God will give you whatever you ask." ²³Jesus said to her, "Your brother will rise again." ²⁴Martha answered, "I know he will rise again in the resurrection at the last day." ²⁵Jesus said to her, "I am the resurrection and the life. The one who believes in me will live, even though they die; ²⁶and whoever lives by believing in me will never die. Do you believe this?" ²⁷"Yes, Lord," she replied, "I believe that you are the Messiah, the Son of God, who is to come into the world." ²⁸After she had said this, she went back and called her sister Mary aside. "The Teacher is here," she said, "and is asking for you." ²⁹When Mary heard this, she got up quickly and went to him. ³⁰Now Jesus had not yet entered the village, but was still at the place where Martha had met him. ³¹When the Jews who had been with Mary in the house, comforting her, noticed how quickly she got up and went out, they followed her, supposing she was going to the tomb to mourn there. ³²When Mary reached the place where Jesus was and saw him, she fell at his feet and said, "Lord, if you had been here, my brother would not have died." ³³When Jesus saw her weeping, and the Jews who had come along with her also weeping, he was deeply moved in spirit and troubled. ³⁴"Where have you laid him?" he asked. "Come and see, Lord," they replied. ³⁵Jesus wept. ³⁶Then the Jews said, "See how he loved him!" ³⁷But some of them said, "Could not he who opened the eyes of the blind man have kept

John 11:38-44 (ESV) Jesus Raises Lazarus ³⁸Then Jesus, deeply moved again, came to the tomb. It was a cave, and a stone lay against it. ³⁹Jesus said, "Take away the stone." Martha, the sister of the dead man, said to him, "Lord, by this time there will be an odor, for he has been dead four days." ⁴⁰Jesus said to her, "Did I not tell you that if you believed you would see the glory of God?" ⁴¹So they took away the stone. And Jesus lifted up his eyes and said, "Father, I thank you that you have heard me. ⁴²I knew that you always hear me, but I said this on account of the people standing around, that they may believe that you sent me." ⁴³When he had said these things, he cried out with a loud voice, "Lazarus, come out." ⁴⁴The man who had died came out, his hands and feet bound with linen strips, and his face wrapped with a cloth. Jesus said to them, "Unbind him, and let him go."

John 11: 45 (NLT) The Plot to Kill Jesus

⁴⁵Many of the people who were with Mary believed in Jesus when they saw this happen.

34

Jesus Restores Sight to Bartimaeus in Jericho

Matthew 20:29-34 (NIV) [29]As Jesus and his disciples were leaving Jericho, a large crowd followed him. [30]Two blind men were sitting by the roadside, and when they heard that Jesus was going by, they shouted, "Lord, Son of David, have mercy on us!" [31]The crowd rebuked them and told them to be quiet, but they shouted all the louder, "Lord, Son of David, have mercy on us!" [32]Jesus stopped and called them. "What do you want me to do for you?" he asked. [33]"Lord," they answered, "we want our sight." [34]Jesus had compassion on them and touched their eyes. Immediately they received their sight and followed him.

Mark 10:46-52 (ESV) [46]And they came to Jericho. And as he was leaving Jericho with his disciples and a great crowd, Bartimaeus, a blind beggar, the son of Timaeus, was sitting by the roadside. [47]And when he heard that it was Jesus of Nazareth, he began to cry out and say, "Jesus, Son of David, have mercy on me!" [48]And many rebuked him, telling him to be silent. But he cried out all the more, "Son of David, have mercy on me!" [49]And Jesus stopped and said, "Call him." And they called the blind man, saying to him, "Take heart. Get up; he is calling you." [50]And throwing off his cloak, he sprang up and came to Jesus. [51]And Jesus said to him, "What do you want me to do for you?" And the blind man said to him, "Rabbi, let me recover my sight." [52]And Jesus said to him, "Go your way; your faith has made you well." And immediately he recovered his sight and followed him on the way.

Luke 18:35-43 (NET) [35]As Jesus approached Jericho, a blind man was sitting by the road begging. [36]When he heard a crowd going by, he asked what was going on. [37]They told him, "Jesus the Nazarene is passing by." [38]So he called out, "Jesus, Son of David, have mercy on me!" [39]And those who were in front scolded him to get him to be quiet, but he shouted even more, "Son of David, have mercy on me!" [40]So Jesus stopped and ordered the beggar to be brought to him. When the man came near, Jesus asked him, [41]"What do you want me to do for you?" He replied, "Lord, let me see again." [42]Jesus said to him, "Receive your sight; your faith has healed you." [43]And immediately he regained his sight and followed Jesus, praising God. When all the people saw it, they too gave praise to God.

35

Jesus Withers the Fig Tree
on the Road from Bethany

Matthew 21:18-22 (NLT) [18]In the morning, as Jesus was returning to Jerusalem, he was hungry, [19]and he noticed a fig tree beside the road. He went over to see if there were any figs, but there were only leaves. Then he said to it, "May you never bear fruit again!" And immediately the fig tree withered up. [20]The disciples were amazed when they saw this and asked, "How did the fig tree wither so quickly?" [21]Then Jesus told them, "I tell you the truth, if you have faith and don't doubt, you can do things like this and much more. You can even say to this mountain, 'May you be lifted up and thrown into the sea,' and it will happen. [22]You can pray for anything, and if you have faith, you will receive it."

Mark 11:12-14 (NIV) [12]The next day as they were leaving Bethany, Jesus was hungry. [13]Seeing in the distance a fig tree in leaf, he went to find out if it had any fruit. When he reached it, he found nothing but leaves, because it was not the season for figs. [14]Then he said to the tree, "May no one ever eat fruit from you again." And his disciples heard him say it.

36

Jesus Heals a Servant's Severed Ear While He Is Being Arrested

Luke 22:50-51 (ESV) [50]And one of them struck the servant of the high priest and cut off his right ear. [51]But Jesus said, "No more of this!" And he touched his ear and healed him.

37

The Second Miraculous Catch
of Fish at the Sea of Tiberias

John 21:4-11 (NET) [4]When it was already very early morning, Jesus stood on the beach, but the disciples did not know that it was Jesus. [5]So Jesus said to them, "Children, you don't have any fish, do you?" They replied, "No." [6]He told them, "Throw your net on the right side of the boat, and you will find some." So they threw the net, and were not able to pull it in because of the large number of fish. [7]Then the disciple whom Jesus loved said to Peter, "It is the Lord!" So Simon Peter, when he heard that it was the Lord, tucked in his outer garment (for he had nothing on underneath it), and plunged into the sea. [8]Meanwhile the other disciples came with the boat, dragging the net full of fish, for they were not far from land, only about a hundred yards. [9]When they got out on the beach, they saw a charcoal fire ready with a fish placed on it, and bread. [10]Jesus said, "Bring some of the fish you have just now caught." [11]So Simon Peter went aboard and pulled the net to shore. It was full of large fish, 153, but although there were so many, the net was not torn.

Miracles of the Apostles of Jesus

All the Apostles of Jesus were ordinary men, with no exceptions.

> "[13]The members of the council were amazed when they saw the boldness of Peter and John, for they could see that they were ordinary men with no special training in the Scriptures. They also recognized them as men who had been with Jesus" **Acts 4:13 (NLT)**

Like us, they had personal strengths and weaknesses and both good and bad days. Some were simple fishermen (*e.g.* Peter, Andrew, James and John), one a despised tax collector (*i.e.* Matthew), one a murderous zealot trusting in Judaism (*i.e.* Paul), etc; and all were very young, strong men. In short, all of Jesus' apostles were sinners saved by the grace of God.

God prepared some amazing miracles for these men to perform at the most crucial time in the establishment of Christ's Church.

> "[10] For we are God's handiwork, created in Christ Jesus to do good works, which God prepared in advance for us to do." **Ephesians 2:10 (NIV)**

Don't ever forget the biblical truth, "ALL miracles are God's miracles."

Early in Jesus' ministry, not long after choosing his twelve disciples, he commissioned his apostles for a short mission to the Jews, *"Go and announce to them that the Kingdom of Heaven is near. Heal the sick, raise the dead, cure those with leprosy, and cast out demons. Give as freely as you have received!"*.

" ⁷And proclaim as you go, saying, 'The kingdom of heaven is at hand. ⁸Heal the sick, raise the dead, cleanse lepers, cast out demons. You received without paying; give without pay." **Matthew 10:7-8 (ESV)**

The disciples followed instructions and returned, sharing about all the great miracles they performed.

"¹⁰When the apostles returned, they told Jesus everything they had done. Then he took them with him and they withdrew privately to a town called Bethsaida." **Luke 9:10 (NET)**

Soon, Jesus sent seventy-two disciples from his broader following on a similar mission.

"The Lord now chose seventy-two other disciples and sent them ahead in pairs to all the towns and places he planned to visit." **Luke 10:1 (NLT)**

"¹⁷The seventy-two returned with joy and said, "Lord, even the demons submit to us in your name." Luke 10:17 (NIV).

"²⁰Nevertheless, do not rejoice in this, that the spirits are subject to you, but rejoice that your names are written in heaven."" Luke 10:20 (ESV)

One can only imagine the great miracles the disciples performed during these short mission trips.

"¹²So they went out and preached that all should repent. ¹³They cast out many demons and anointed many sick people with olive oil and healed them." **Mark 6:12-13 (NET)**

However, the Lord did gift us with the Bible's Acts of the Apostles, which we can search for the accounted miracles of the apostles.

Peter tells us why the apostles had these extraordinary powers, "And the Father, as he promised, gave Jesus the Holy Spirit to pour out upon us, just as you see and hear today"

> "³³Now he is exalted to the place of highest honor in heaven, at God's right hand. And the Father, as he had promised, gave him the Holy Spirit to pour out upon us, just as you see and hear today." **Acts 2:33 (NLT)**

We'll start the list with a miracle Peter performed on the Sea of Galilee.

List of miracles of the Apostles of Jesus

Miracles	
Peter walked on water	Matthew 14:28-31
All believers spoke in foreign languages	Acts 2:4
Many signs and wonders performed	Acts 2:43; 5:1-12
Peter and John healed the lame man	Acts 3:1-11; 3:16
Peter's shadow fell on the sick, healing them	Acts 5:15-16
Stephen performed amazing miracles and signs	Acts 6:8-10
Philip cast out demons and healed the lame	Acts 8:7; 8:13
Peter & John laid hands on believers who then received the Holy Spirit	Acts 8:14-17

Peter healed the lame Aeneas in Lydda	Acts 9:32-35
Peter raised Tabitha, aka Dorcas, from the dead	Acts 9:36-43
Paul cursed and blinded the blasphemous Elymas the sorcerer	Acts 13:11-12
Paul and Barnabas performed signs and wonders in Iconium	Acts 14:1-3
Paul and Barnabas healed the crippled man who had faith	Acts 14:8-10
Paul and Silas cast a demon out of a fortune telling slave girl	Acts 16:16-18
Paul given extreme power for many unusual miracles. People touched him with aprons and handkerchiefs and laid the cloths on the sick and demon-possessed, who were then healed.	Acts 19:10 -12
Paul raised Eutychus from the dead after a terrible accident	Acts 20:9-12
Paul was unharmed by poisonous a snake bite in Malta	Acts 28:1-6
Paul healed Publius' father of fever and dysentery	Acts 28: 7-8
Paul healed all the sick people on the island of Malta	Acts 28:9-10

APOSTLES'
MIRACLES

01

Peter walked on water (Matthew 14:28-31, NIV)
²⁸"Lord, if it's you," Peter replied, "tell me to come to you on the water." ²⁹"Come," he said. Then Peter got down out of the boat, walked on the water and came toward Jesus. ³⁰But when he saw the wind, he was afraid and, beginning to sink, cried out, "Lord, save me!" ³¹Immediately Jesus reached out his hand and caught him. "You of little faith," he said, "why did you doubt?"

02

All believers spoke in foreign languages (Acts 2:2-4, ESV) When the day of Pentecost arrived, they were all together in one place. ²And suddenly there came from heaven a sound like a mighty rushing wind, and it filled the entire house where they were sitting. ³And divided tongues as of fire appeared to them and rested on each one of them. ⁴And they were all filled with the Holy Spirit and began to speak in other tongues as the Spirit gave them utterance.

03

Many signs and wonders performed (Acts 2:43, NET) ⁴³Reverential awe came over everyone, and many wonders and miraculous signs came about by the apostles. **(Acts 5: 1-12, NLT)** But there was a certain man named Ananias who, with his wife, Sapphira, sold some property. ²He brought part of the money to the apostles, claiming it was the full amount. With his wife's consent, he kept the rest. ³Then Peter said, "Ananias, why have you let Satan fill your heart? You lied to the Holy Spirit, and you kept some of the money for yourself. ⁴The property was yours to sell or not sell, as you wished. And after selling it, the money was also yours to give away. How could you do a thing like this? You weren't lying to us but to God!" ⁵As soon as Ananias heard these words, he fell to the floor and died. Everyone who heard about it was terrified. ⁶Then some young men got up, wrapped him in a sheet, and took him out and buried him. ⁷About three hours later his wife came in, not knowing what had happened. ⁸Peter asked her, "Was this the price you and your husband received for your land?" "Yes," she replied, "that was the price." ⁹And Peter said, "How could the two of you even think of conspiring to test the Spirit of the Lord like this? The young men who buried your husband are just outside the door, and they will carry you out, too." [10]Instantly, she fell to the floor and died. When the young men came in and saw that she was dead, they carried her out and buried her beside her husband. [11]Great fear gripped the entire church and everyone else who heard what had happened. The Apostles Heal Many [12]The apostles were performing many miraculous signs and wonders among the people. And all the believers were meeting regularly at the Temple in the area known as Solomon's Colonnade.

04

Peter and John healed the lame man (Acts 3:1-11; 3:16, NIV) One day Peter and John were going up to the temple at the time of prayer—at three in the afternoon. [2]Now a man who was lame from birth was being carried to the temple gate called Beautiful, where he was put every day to beg from those going into the temple courts. [3]When he saw Peter and John about to enter, he asked them for money. [4]Peter looked straight at him, as did John. Then Peter said, "Look at us!" [5]So the man gave them his attention, expecting to get something from them. [6]Then Peter said, "Silver or gold I do not have, but what I do have I give you. In the name of Jesus Christ of Nazareth, walk." [7]Taking him by the right hand, he helped him up, and instantly the man's feet and ankles became strong. [8]He jumped to his feet and began to walk. Then he went with them into the temple courts, walking and jumping, and praising God. [9]When all the people saw him walking and praising God, [10]they recognized him as the same man who used to sit begging at the temple gate called Beautiful, and they were filled with wonder and amazement at what had happened to him. [11]While the man held on to Peter and John, all the people were astonished and came running to them in the place called Solomon's Colonnade.[16]By faith in the name of Jesus, this man whom you see and know was made strong. It is Jesus' name and the faith that comes through him that has completely healed him, as you can all see.

Peter's shadow fell on the sick, healing them (Acts 5:15-16, ESV) [15]so that they even carried out the sick into the streets and laid them on cots and mats, that as Peter came by at least his shadow might fall on some of them. [16]The people also gathered from the towns around Jerusalem, bringing the sick and those afflicted with unclean spirits, and they were all healed.

Stephen performed amazing miracles and signs (Acts 6:8-10, NET) [8]Now Stephen, full of grace and power, was performing great wonders and miraculous signs among the people. [9]But some men from the Synagogue of the Freedmen (as it was called), both Cyrenians and Alexandrians, as well as some from Cilicia and the province of Asia, stood up and argued with Stephen. [10]Yet they were not able to resist the wisdom and the Spirit with which he spoke.

07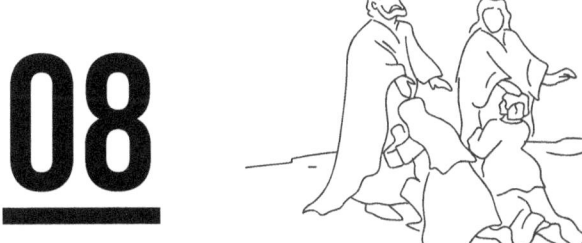

Philip cast out demons and healed the lame (Acts 8:7; 8:13, NLT) [7] Many evil spirits were cast out, screaming as they left their victims. And many who had been paralyzed or lame were healed.

(Acts 8:13, NIV) [13]Simon himself believed and was baptized. And he followed Philip everywhere, astonished by the great signs and miracles he saw.

08

Peter and John laid hands on believers who then received the Holy Spirit (Acts 8:14-17, ESV) [14]Now when the apostles at Jerusalem heard that Samaria had received the word of God, they sent to them Peter and John, [15]who came down and prayed for them that they might receive the Holy Spirit, [16]for he had not yet fallen on any of them, but they had only been baptized in the name of the Lord Jesus. [17]Then they laid their hands on them and they received the Holy Spirit.

Peter healed lame Aeneas in Lydda (Acts 9:32-35, NET) ³²Now as Peter was traveling around from place to place, he also came down to the saints who lived in Lydda. ³³He found there a man named Aeneas who had been confined to a mattress for eight years because he was paralyzed. ³⁴Peter said to him, "Aeneas, Jesus the Christ heals you. Get up and make your own bed!" And immediately he got up. ³⁵All those who lived in Lydda and Sharon saw him, and they turned to the Lord.

Peter raised Tabitha, aka Dorcas, from the dead (Acts 9:36-43, NLT) ³⁶There was a believer in Joppa named Tabitha (which in Greek is Dorcas). She was always doing kind things for others and helping the poor. ³⁷About this time she became ill and died. Her body was washed for burial and laid in an upstairs room. ³⁸But the believers had heard that Peter was nearby at Lydda, so they sent two men to beg him, "Please come as soon as possible!" ³⁹So Peter returned with them; and as soon as he arrived, they took him to the upstairs room. The room was filled with widows who were weeping and showing him the coats and other clothes Dorcas had made for them. ⁴⁰But Peter asked them all to leave the room; then he knelt and prayed. Turning to the body he said, "Get up, Tabitha." And she opened her eyes! When she saw Peter, she sat up! [41]He gave her his hand and helped her up. Then he called in the widows and all the believers, and he presented her to them alive. [42]The news spread through the whole town, and many believed in the Lord. [43]And Peter stayed a long time in Joppa, living with Simon, a tanner of hides.

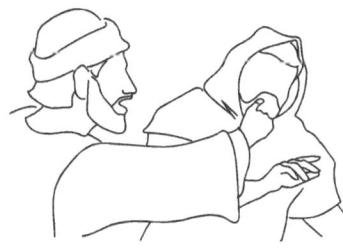

Paul cursed and blinded the blasphemous Elymas the sorcerer (Acts 13:11-12, NIV) [11]Now the hand of the Lord is against you. You are going to be blind for a time, not even able to see the light of the sun." Immediately mist and darkness came over him, and he groped about, seeking someone to lead him by the hand. [12]When the proconsul saw what had happened, he believed, for he was amazed at the teaching about the Lord.

Paul and Barnabas performed signs and wonders in Iconium (Acts 14:1-3, ESV) [1]Now at Iconium they entered together into the Jewish synagogue and spoke in such a way that a great number of both Jews and Greeks believed. [2]But the unbelieving Jews stirred up the Gentiles and poisoned their minds against the brothers. [3]So they remained for a long time, speaking boldly for the Lord, who bore witness to the word of his grace, granting signs and wonders to be done by their hands.

Paul and Barnabas healed the crippled man who had faith (Acts 14:8-10, NET) [8] In Lystra sat a man who could not use his feet, lame from birth, who had never walked. [9] This man was listening to Paul as he was speaking. When Paul stared intently at him and saw he had faith to be healed, [10] he said with a loud voice, "Stand upright on your feet." And the man leaped up and began walking.

Paul and Silas cast a demon out of a fortune-telling slave girl (Acts 16:16-18, NLT) [16]One day as we were going down to the place of prayer, we met a slave girl who had a spirit that enabled her to tell the future. She earned a lot of money for her masters by telling fortunes. [17]She followed Paul and the rest of us, shouting, "These men are servants of the Most High God, and they have come to tell you how to be saved." [18]This went on day after day until Paul got so exasperated that he turned and said to the demon within her, "I command you in the name of Jesus Christ to come out of her." And instantly it left her.

15

Paul given extreme power for many unusual miracles. People touched him with aprons and handkerchiefs and laid the cloths on the sick and demon-possessed, who were then healed. (Acts 19:10-12, NIV)
¹⁰This went on for two years, so that all the Jews and Greeks who lived in the province of Asia heard the word of the Lord. ¹¹God did extraordinary miracles through Paul, ¹²so that even handkerchiefs and aprons that had touched him were taken to the sick, and their illnesses were cured and the evil spirits left them.

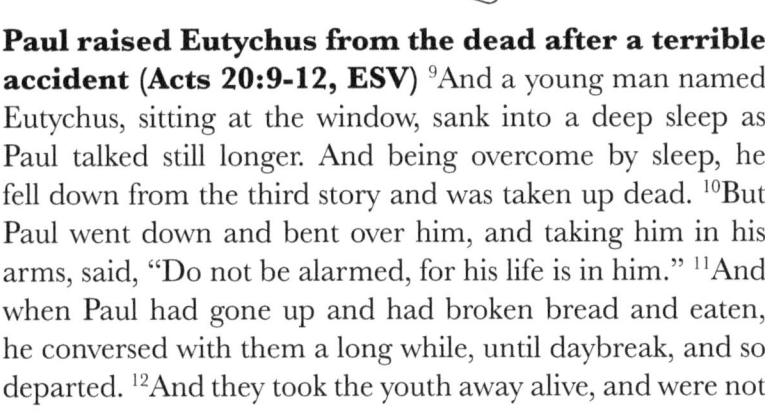

16

Paul raised Eutychus from the dead after a terrible accident (Acts 20:9-12, ESV) ⁹And a young man named Eutychus, sitting at the window, sank into a deep sleep as Paul talked still longer. And being overcome by sleep, he fell down from the third story and was taken up dead. ¹⁰But Paul went down and bent over him, and taking him in his arms, said, "Do not be alarmed, for his life is in him." ¹¹And when Paul had gone up and had broken bread and eaten, he conversed with them a long while, until daybreak, and so departed. ¹²And they took the youth away alive, and were not a little comforted.

17

Paul unharmed by a poisonous snake bite in Malta (Acts 28:1-6, NET) [1]After we had safely reached shore, we learned that the island was called Malta. [2]The local inhabitants showed us extraordinary kindness, for they built a fire and welcomed us all because it had started to rain and was cold. [3]When Paul had gathered a bundle of brushwood and was putting it on the fire, a viper came out because of the heat and fastened itself on his hand. [4]When the local people saw the creature hanging from Paul's hand, they said to one another, "No doubt this man is a murderer! Although he has escaped from the sea, Justice herself has not allowed him to live!" [5]However, Paul shook the creature off into the fire and suffered no harm. [6]But they were expecting that he was going to swell up or suddenly drop dead. So after they had waited a long time and had seen nothing unusual happen to him, they changed their minds and said he was a god.

18

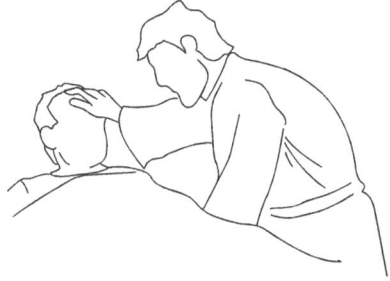

Paul healed Publius' father of fever and dysentery (Acts 28:7-8, NLT) [7]Near the shore where we landed was an estate belonging to Publius, the chief official of the island. He welcomed us and treated us kindly for three days. [8]As it happened, Publius's father was ill with fever and dysentery. Paul went in and prayed for him, and laying his hands on him, he healed him.

Paul healed all the sick people on the island of Malta (Acts 28:9-10, NIV) [9]When this had happened, the rest of the sick on the island came and were cured. [10] They honored us in many ways; and when we were ready to sail, they furnished us with the supplies we needed.

Reasons for the Apostles' Miracles

The main reasons for Jesus performing his own miracles were to glorify God the Father and announce that the Kingdom of God had arrived in the flesh (i.e., the Son of God). Both the teachings and miracles of Jesus were witnesses to who He truly is, the Son of God and Savior of the world. **(John 5:36)**

In essence, Christ's miracles happened to be an expression of salvation. Is there any reason to think that Jesus' apostles had differing reasons for their miracles? Not at all. The reasons for the apostles performing miracles were to glorify God and his Son, and also the Kingdom of God. **Miracles are attention-getters and great works of authorization for the gospel message, of which the apostles were the prime conveyors.**

Both the apostles and the gospel needed authentication, which the amazing signs, wonders, and miracles provided in full. **(Acts 14:3)**

The apostles' miracles verified the gospel message, which says that Jesus forgives the sins of those who repent and believe in him. **(Acts 17:30-31)**

Here is the commissioning statement Jesus gave his messengers, "But you will receive power when the Holy Spirit has come upon you. You will be my witnesses in Jerusalem, in all Judea and Samaria, and to the uttermost parts of the earth." **(Acts 1:8)**

The miracles are truly performed by the Holy Spirit, not the apostles, so again, to whom should the glory be directed? That's right, to God Almighty.

Jesus said, "Truly, truly, I tell you, he who believes in me, the works that I do, he will do also; and he will do greater works than these, because I am going to the Father. And whatever you ask in my name, this I will do, that the Father may be glorified in the Son." **(John 14:12-13)**

Miracles also brought fear into the hearts of people. When God struck and killed Ananias and Sapphira through Peter, great fear swept through the hearts of both believers and unbelievers. **God's immense power, demonstrated in the apostle's miracles, was causing great fear and chaos throughout Jerusalem and the surrounding area. (Acts 5:1-11)**

Another critical reason for why God worked miracles through His apostles was to strengthen the believers. Further, Paul told the Corinthians directly that he wanted them to repent of their impurity, sexual immorality, and lustful pleasures. In other words, Paul, his message, and his challenge was for his listeners to hear and believe the message, and prove it through their obedience to God. Obedience to the Scriptures leads to a strong spiritual life.

Still, today, in all these ways and for all these reasons God showed His greatness through miracles. First, through the Prophets of old, like Moses and Elijah; then through Jesus Himself; and finally, through Jesus' apostles. **These miracles are for your benefit, so that you are drawn to God through His Son, Jesus.** That fact should make you feel important, because you really are.

Denying God's miracles, since they are His, is denying God himself. Denying God's Miracles, is denying his Son. Denying God's Miracles, is denying and blaspheming the Holy Spirit, which is the ONLY unforgivable sin. Denying God's miracles also denies his Holy Word, the Bible. **(Mark 8:38)**

In fact, denying God's miracles is equivalent to calling God a liar and results in the eternal destruction of your soul.

²⁰Then Jesus began to denounce the towns where he had done so many of his miracles, because they hadn't repented of their sins and turned to God. ²¹"What sorrow awaits you, Korazin and Bethsaida! For if the miracles I did in you had been done in wicked Tyre and Sidon, their people would have repented of their sins long ago, clothing themselves in burlap and throwing ashes on their heads to show their remorse. ²²I tell you, Tyre and Sidon will be better off on judgment day than you. ²³"And you people of Capernaum, will you be honored in heaven? No, you will go down to the place of the dead. For if the miracles I did for you had been done in wicked Sodom, it would still be here today. ²⁴I tell you, even Sodom will be better off on judgment day than you." (**Matthew 11:20-24, NLT**)

²⁴If I had not done among them the works that no one else did, they would not be guilty of sin, but now they have seen and hated both me and my Father. (**John 15:24, ESV**)

The following verse is critical for understanding why God worked miracles through His apostles:

¹Therefore we must pay closer attention to what we have heard, so that we do not drift away. ²For if the message spoken through angels proved to be so firm that every violation or disobedience received its just penalty, ³how will we escape if we neglect such a great salvation? It was first communicated through the Lord and was confirmed to us by those who heard him, ⁴while God confirmed their witness with signs and wonders and various miracles and gifts of the Holy Spirit distributed according to his will. (**Hebrews 2:1-4, NET**)

There's a message that God wants to spread around the world, and this is it: **The Good News proclaims that Jesus Christ died for our sins. All those who repent and believe in His name will be saved.**

Not to diminish God's miracles, but the most important thing to grasp is God's gospel of love and forgiveness. The supernatural phenomenon of miracles is spectacular and glorifies the Lord; however, the salvation of a spiritually dead sinner by God's grace is His greatest miracle, which Jesus' Apostles would wholeheartedly affirm.

Has it sunk deep into your soul yet? **Do you realize that you must experience God's forgiveness ABOVE ALL ELSE?**

If so, and you've been saved, you're blessed, because not many people do come to realize God's amazing miracle of salvation. This leads us to the second most critical thing in your life. You're called not simply to receive God's forgiveness, but to proclaim the same gospel to the rest of the world.

Bible Verses of the Miracles of the Apostles of Jesus

[1]"I am the true vine, and my Father is the gardener. [2]He cuts off every branch in me that bears no fruit, while every branch that does bear fruit he prunes so that it will be even more fruitful. [3]You are already clean because of the word I have spoken to you. [4]Remain in me, as I also remain in you. No branch can bear fruit by itself; it must remain in the vine. Neither can you bear fruit unless you remain in me. [5]"I am the vine; you are the branches. If you remain in me and I in you, you will bear much fruit; apart from me you can do nothing. **(John 15:1-5, NIV)**

[18]And Jesus came and said to them, "All authority in heaven and on earth has been given to me. [19]Go therefore and make disciples of all nations, baptizing them in the name of the Father and of the Son and of the Holy Spirit, [20]teaching them to observe all that I have commanded you. And behold, I am with you always, to the end of the age."**(Matthew 28:18-20, ESV)**

Miracle Prayer

Dear Lord, we bow before You, fully amazed at Your awesome power. We deserve ruin because of our sin, but You have grace and mercy on us, O God. Forgive us of our rebellious nature and unrighteous ways. Heal us from the disease You call sin. In Jesus Christ we pray, Amen.

S. Alfred Cherubim
Senior Pastor
Redeemer Christ Assembly
Brampton
CANADA

MORE FROM PASTOR ALFRED

PASTOR • SERVANT • AUTHOR

alfred-cherubim.com

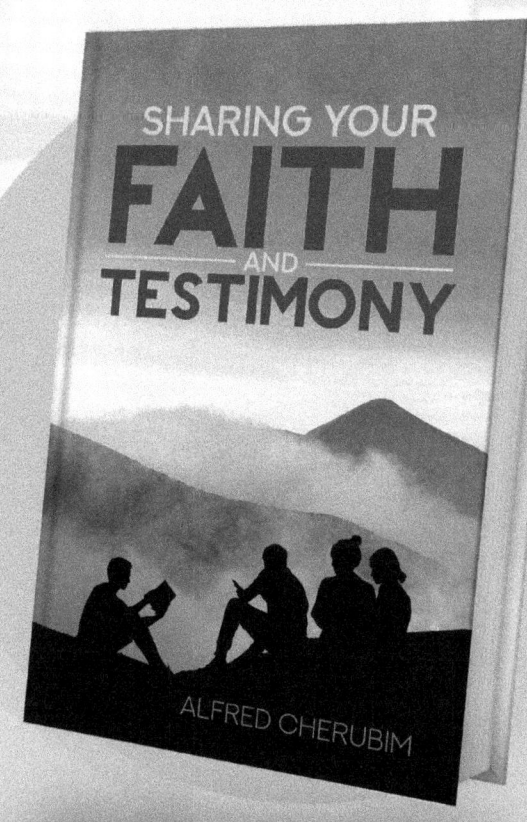